QUIT MANAGING and START COACHING

D1158976

TIM HAGEN

ISBN: 1-4392-3290-3
ISBN-13: 9781439232903

Visit www.booksurge.com to order additional copies.

CONTENTS

Foreword

Coaching...when I think of coaching, I used to think only of Vince Lombardi, Adolf Rupp, John Wooden, Bill Walsh, and today...Bill Belichick comes to mind. The journey we have been on the past several years has transformed our culture from a pass/fail culture to a developmental culture. I now view each of our managers as coaches as well. Becoming an effective coach leaves much more of an imprint and legacy with your staff than just managing them. The Sales Progress program is an easy-to-learn system that can transform your culture too.

Marc Holland, CSI, CDT
Executive Vice President of Sales and Marketing
InPro Corporation

Introduction

I struggled with this book, because so much time is needed to write such a book and I would rather be out there building coaches at client sites. Yes, we provide coaching services, but many people encouraged me to write a book and this is the main reason I did so. It's a book about a coaching methodology and system—versus simply being a book about coaching concepts.

Coaching has gained such publicity in recent years with many authors and experts leveraging this movement. There are some great coaching books on the market and there are also books that speak conceptually and ambiguously. I promise, when you finish reading this book, you will walk away with multiple ideas on how to go about coaching.

In this book you will learn a specific methodology and system that will provide unlimited choices to deliver coaching services to your employees. The methodology is called Progress Coaching. It's called that for one simple reason: you coach people to progress. That's it!

Why Coaching?

First, we need it. Plain and simple, we need to build performance EVERY DAY in business and our people. Yet coaching, even with its recent popular movement, all too often becomes a cliché inside organizations. To be successful, coaching must be a dedicated effort and one that is measured along the way.

The main difference you will have to distinguish on your own is the difference between management and coaching. We define coaching as the means to driving better performance. Management includes endeavors that require leadership and directives to employees. There is some grey area between the two—depending on the organization.

Here is an example: If an employee is continuously late for work, it's probably going to be a management issue. There is not really a performance issue per se. An employee who misses deadlines may be lacking time management skills, which lead to the missing of deadlines— this is probably a performance-based issue. The key to understanding the value of why we need to coach is that ALL employees can improve performance. We never really hit perfection.

Management often struggles with the concept of coaching and how to go about coaching due to two main issues:

- First, it's easier to just dictate to employees and not engage as much because it saves time (Wrong).

- Second, managers have a fear of coaching. The fear could be that they do not have time to coach, they might end up being vulnerable in front of employees, or they feel unequipped to effectively conduct coaching. All of these fears are common, but they are poor excuses when it comes to developing employees or even evaluating them at the end of the year.

I had an epiphany at a client site when I walked into a building about six years ago and noticed the culture was very quiet, almost weird with silence. I asked a manager I was working with what was going on. He told me all the managers' end-of-the-year evaluations were due in the Human Resources department by 11:00 a.m.

I walked around the building and noticed every manager was writing vigorously. I thought, "Wow, how unfair to the employees—managers are rushing to get a document done within minutes that covered the last year."

I also knew the company had no coaching program. The employees were being evaluated by managers who were not engaged with them or coaching them to perform better and receive a good end-of-the-year evaluations.

Coaching is also required because traditional training, such as workshops or seminars, has exonerated management from its responsibility to build employee careers. As you will see in the research section of this book, traditional training by itself is not very effective, but when it's combined with coaching, it produces four times the results compared to training by itself.

Plain and simple, we need to coach our employees to produce better-performing employees and organizations. This presents a great opportunity to gain a competitive edge in the marketplace—developing employees should not be difficult.

Coaching is a tool to promote greatness in all of us, but few managers truly possess the knowledge and skills to drive the coaching process. This book is about providing insight into a process called *Progress Coaching*—this is our process of coaching employees to progress.

"I lost that deal because I did not handle their price objection effectively."

The issue is not that employees lie, but do we create an environment where people are comfortable communicating bad news? Studies have shown that roughly 50 percent of all salespeople do not hit their sales quotas; therefore, when managers are in a meeting and everyone nods when asked if they are going to hit their numbers...guess what? Something is very wrong. Coaching allows you to know where and when this will not occur. The important thing is that coaching gets you involved in the process of fixing the problem.

Keys to Coaching Success

Managers who value coaching admit that they need to be better coaches—"better" in terms of methods and techniques that truly drive change in their employees' performance. Most coaching in the industry is about feeling good or earning the right to coach...Bull. We need to do it because performance driving benefits the organizations, its leaders, and, most importantly, the employees. If we have high-performing employees, we in turn will have ecstatic customers and better organizational bottom lines.

The keys to coaching are simple:

1. Managers develop skill sets they can take anywhere in the organization.

2. Employees learn they can get better each and every day.

3. Departments can grow to improve employee learning and become more cooperative with one another.

4. Organizations drive the bottom line with managers coaching employees and employees working together in a culture that progresses every day.

5. Last, an absolute willingness to get better at every level within the organization.

Management   ✂   (Grey Area)   ✂   Coaching

Leveraging the real world is critical to gaining "buy in" when coaching people. They will be more open to learning if it positively affects their real world. It's one of the big challenges traditional training has yet to solve.

Workshops and seminars traditionally do not address specific attributes of what truly challenges people. Coaching allows managers and leaders to not only coach their employees but also produce results in the real world. For example, a form of traditional training is a salesperson going to a seminar on closing skills. A coach would role-play as it relates to a specific perspective; therefore, if the deal is won, the salesperson will see how the coaching produces real-world results. This will lead people to engage more in the coaching process because they personally benefit.

Use SDL (Self-Directed Learning) as a tool to accelerate the coaching process. Self-Directed Learning is a powerful tool when developing employees. Employees actually prefer to learn on their own versus attending large training sessions. If we take the time to structure self-directed learning programs and ultimately combine them with other coaching methods, employees' development accelerates exponentially. The key is to take the time to design activities that will produce the desired results (see examples later in this book).

How Coaching Will be Successful

Coaching is successful when performance progresses—each employee will progress in different ways. People need to realize they can always be better at something, and managers must realize there is tremendous gain in having employees who are developing and progressing. The key to successful coaching is a willing participant and coach.

Steps to be taken include setting expectations, defining desired results, and creating mutually beneficial goals. The manager (coach) and employee essentially work together to develop better performance.

The keys to successful coaching are quite simple:

1. Create understanding of desired performance improvement.

2. Structure a consistently scheduled coaching program.

3. Promote the simulation or practice of the desired performance.

4. Recognize and reward effort—for effort is required to eventually attain any type of results.

5. Have the employee complete the learning assignment; otherwise, the coach may interpret the lack of completion as a sign that the employee in not interested in attaining better performance.

What Areas Do We Need to Coach?

There are two main areas to keep in mind when coaching employees—each area will dictate the coaching content and delivery. This is critical to understanding how to leverage the Progress Coaching process. The two areas depict specific elements that will accelerate the coaching process:

1. Functional Requirements – Functional requirements are those attributes that we functionally require. These are NOT things found on a job description; rather, they are areas that are specifically required to successfully do a job. For example, a job description would simply list "cold calling" as an area in a job description.

A functional requirement would be "Cold call with absolute energy and passion for every phone call." The key is to provide an adjective with specific requirements that deliver performance. You can also have multiple functional requirements surrounding one area like cold calling. For example, a second functional requirement involving cold calling could be "Handle competitor objections on every cold call with flair, confidence, and conviction for driving value."

The key to writing functional requirements is to be specific, add an adjective, and categorize it within a tier of learning—the learning tier is either knowledge, skills, behavior, or creativity. Most managers would simply send their staff to a cold calling workshop. But what if half the staff has never made cold calls (lacks knowledge and skills) and the other half has a genuine fear due to rejection (behaviorally challenged)? The problem is we often take a generic approach to developing staff around the topic when, in fact, there are many elements that affect the way we need to learn.

2. Four Tiers of Learning – K, S, B, C — As mentioned previously, it's critical to place your functional requirements into categories that we call the Four Tiers of Learning. When you look at what's required to be successful at various jobs, you will see a collage of knowledge, skills, behaviors, and creative elements.

For example, let's say a customer service job requires someone to answer the phones and deliver proper information (knowledge) about a company's products. In addition, the employee must be friendly and deliver great customer service. One employee may lack proper product knowledge, while another employee may have enough product knowledge, but comes off as rude and short with customers. In addition, the second employee states he or she is doing the job well enough. The first employee is lacking product knoweldge and the second employee is lacking a true behavioral commitment to delivering great customer service.

Now, would you really send both of these people to the same workshop? Would you really coach these people the same way? Of course not! That's where the Progress Coaching System comes in. If you define your functional requirements and categorize them into the Four Tiers of Learning, you are way ahead of any generic coaching concept.

The following definitions also provide examples of the Four Tiers of Learning:

Knowledge – to know or understand. Examples could be internal processes, product knowledge, technical attributes, etc.

Skills – to be able to perform or do something specifically. A skill could be active listening, closing for sales people, negotiating, etc.

Behavior – to execute without fear or anxiety—and consistently without thinking. Examples could be fear of making cold calls, anxiety with asking for the order, knowing you struggle with active listening, etc.

Creativity – to solve or address situations in nontraditional means.

Note: It is common to have a development area with a combination of learning needs. For example, you may have an employee who does not know how to make a cold call (lack of knowledge), who lacks skills (because there has been no practice), and fears cold calls (lack of confidence).

Why Do Organizations Need Coaching?

There are a number of reasons to develop a coaching organization, but the main objective is to develop employees to perform better. In addition, there are many fundamental reasons why organizations need to coach—it's amazing we do not have more organizations with formal coaching programs. Here is a brief list of reasons why organizations need to coach:

1. Employee retention.

2. Allowing managers to get close to employees' work and solve real-world challenges.

3. Better succession planning due to talent growth.

4. Creating organizational energy.

5. Building coaches within the leadership circles. The more coaches an organization has, the more "performance-improving" employees it will have.

6. Business requires employees to get better. Organizations—with managers who are not coaching their employees—do not have a competitive edge.

7. Employees who experience an increase in skills and work performance actually become more open to change and challenges. This, in itself, is enough to start an organization-wide coaching initiative.

Why Coaching *Unnecessarily* Fails in Organizations

Managers and their general approaches often counter proper coaching principles. For example, when I attended a client's sales meeting, the sales manager got up yelling that they had to hit their numbers and improve their attitudes.

He literally walked out of the meeting feeling it went really well. I responded with, "Yeah, it did, if your goal was to help them start their resumes." He looked at me, startled, and asked, "What do you mean?" The issue was that he never engaged or involved the employees; rather, he talked at them. Nobody really accepts this type of manager effort—if anything, it creates great hallway conversation and gossip.

Why? Because now they have a chance to talk about it; whereas, if the manager had engaged with them using questions to find out how they were feeling, he would have learned a lot more. Instead, he threw things at them and later convinced himself it went well. I had one question for him: "How would you know it went well?"

Managers today are used to telling staff what to do, what they expect, and when it's due. There are certainly times when managers have to do this—as long as they realize this has little to do with performance development. But they are not skilled at developing staff, and in fairness to managers, they have not been properly educated. Managing staff is tough. Hiring people is tough. Having to fire someone is terrible. There are many responsibilities when managing people, and coaching is one that provides a unique opportunity to retain and grow staff. It builds better relationships and higher-performing people within the organization.

What Does Research Show Us about the Need for Coaching?

Research clearly reveals organizational needs for management to become better at coaching. Yes, good managers do not make good coaches. Coaching is about driving performance such as skills, knowledge, behaviors, and creative attributes. Research shows most managers are deficient in driving performance, which is really the opportunity for organizations and their managers to develop a competitive edge over the competition.

The following research reveals some straightforward evidence of why organizations need to coach:

1.   *Leadership Council Stats*

"Engaged employees can yield up to **57 percent** more discretionary effort." – *Corporate Leadership Council (2004)*

"**Eleven percent** of employees are disengaged...**76 percent** are ambivalent at best...only **13 percent** are engaged...but average industry attrition ~**10–12 percent**." – *Corporate Leadership Council (2004)*

Our Own Research

We are not going to mention our client names, for this would not be fair, but here is a brief list of some of their performance challenges when we started working with them:

Client A: The employees never said "thank you" to customers 86 percent of the time—they ended calls with "yup," "all right," "uh huh," etc. It came off insincerely and, quite frankly, it demonstrated a great need for coaching.

Client B: Averaged three and a half close-ended questions for every person in the inside sales force.

Client C: This client had a team of twenty people who all needed to be selling. Half were inside salespeople, and the other half were customer service staff.

Real-World Case Studies

The following case studies do not appear in any order—the objective is to show that coaching works and certain tactics can be used to develop better-performing employees.

1. The Active Listening Nightmare Client

A client's company considered one particular employee to be a fantastic salesperson—she knew products, the industry, and overall selling practices. Management would often praise her depth of industry knowledge and ultimately made assumptions that she was a good salesperson.

In reality, one major development skill challenged her and prevented her from being even an average rep: active listening. Now that may sound harsh, but this employee was every manager's dream employee. She came in early, stayed late, and made as many calls as possible to hit her goal. She was pleasant, devoted, and completely open to getting better—what a person to work with! A coach's dream, but her selling challenge was active listening. She could not wait to get on the phone and talk and talk and talk.

When monitoring her calls, we realized she could not even hear the customer's response, much less the feedback on purchasing. Now, most managers would bring her into the office and say, "Look, you have to slow down and really listen to your customers. It's vital you understand their needs so we can effectively sell our products to them." This approach may seem plausible to some people, but she knew she had a listening problem. Her development was not just skill based; it was behavioral—we needed to break habits that have been forming for years.

Our approach was simple. We told her she was a valued employee and we wanted to really help her move forward. She was excited and eager to do whatever was needed. Now, the team she was on was nervous about coaching, so we asked her for help. We told her some team members could not handle the coaching, and we needed a champion to show the team that coaching was beneficial...she agreed. The threefold approach occurred on a daily basis:

1. She had to turn in a sheet telling her manager two new things she learned about three customers in the morning and three in the afternoon. The only way she could achieve this was to ask questions and be quiet long enough to listen.

2. She attended Friday staff meetings and would only take meeting notes—she could not participate unless she was called on. This eliminated her habit of "talking for the sake of talking."

3. Third, she would meet with us weekly for only twenty minutes. We asked what she was learning by doing this, and most importantly, what was she learning about herself that was beneficial to the selling process. The response was the one we were looking for: She often said, "Gosh, do I talk a lot—I really fight the urge to talk."

Result:

Within six months, her sales rose 105 percent—making 30 percent fewer calls to achieve this result. We never told her she had a terrible active listening challenge; rather, we helped facilitate the experience of listening and asked her some very important questions. First, we asked what she was learning about herself. Second, we asked what she needed to continue to do to maintain the success she was having. On both accounts, she mentioned active listening and that she needed to fight her urge to talk.

Had we started with this approach initially, she would have felt defensive and probably would have closed her mind to learning or even getting better. In summary, I hope you have noticed one major element of this coaching case study: we NEVER told her she needed to get better at active listening.

2. The "Need to Break Through" Manager

One of the toughest things to do when coaching is to get people to break through their fears or barriers. One such manager had a fear of confrontation and willingness to challenge his employees. This manager had many employees under his leadership, but one employee was actually the former department manager. This current manager would literally rant and rave about the former manager, but would later say the situation did not bother him—I knew this not to be true.

After using some of the techniques to be discussed later in this book the manager confronted his fear and the employee. We scripted out how to approach this person and make sure he was confronting the issues and not the person. The interaction went great. The employee stormed out of the room. You are probably asking why did that go great? We learned something very valuable about the employee. She demonstrated a behavior that needed to be dealt with and the manager drew a line in the sand. The employee later left the company probably due to the fact every time she exhibited this behavior, the manager called her on it using specific techniques that required the employee to look in the mirror at herself. The power had shifted and the manager gained tremendous respect from the other employees, all of whom were still employed years later. The negative employee was coached to make a decision based on the betterment of the group. The manager now feels he can coach on any issue.

3. The Apprehensive Manager

A client of ours had over one hundred sales people, but it was a culture where management took a typical approach where results were all that mattered. We struggled to get managers to buy into the coaching concept—they felt they did not have time to coach. I asked "What are you doing as leaders to develop your staff?" Most of the managers struggled to answer this.

The moral of the story: If you do not develop your people, you have made a conscious decision to have your staff remain the same in terms of ability. People do not magically get better unless management helps challenge and drive their performance. Most employees will not arbitrarily choose to get better on their own; if they do, they are usually moved to management.

In this client site, we worked with one manager who was new to the management game. As most of the managers fought the coaching movement, this manager embraced it along with the sales director. In his first months with the staff, he used thirty-second coaching sessions in both the morning and afternoon he did this with two employees. In other words, he spent one minute in the morning and one minute in the afternoon.

The sessions were specific to what they were doing better, and he always used positive adjectives when praising their efforts. Soon, both reps' sales increased by double digits. This manager had a breakthrough by using a simple coaching method most managers will not use. He became a great coach from that point on, and his division always hit its numbers. His staff respected him as his coaching progressed into a more time-invested framework.

Results:

Both employees increased their sales by over 10 percent within a short time. The moral of the case study: Positive reinforcement can take people a long way. It opens the mind for more; whereas, negative reinforcement simply closes the mind to the learning process. Coaching is about leveraging strengths, but most managers focus only on the negatives. If we spent as much—if not more time—on the positives, employees would be more open to working on the areas that need improvement.

4. The Tough Demographic People Ignore

A publicly traded company had secured our services to coach the call center personnel, and I had the privilege of meeting one of my all-time favorite clients. Janet was an employee in her fifties and completely averse to change. Her demographic made it tough on the surface, because she probably looked at me as a younger "hotshot" making money and one who would ask her to do that terrible thing called change. Our first encounter was one I would not wish on anyone—we agreed to meet one-on-one with all staff.

Janet walked in, sat down, folded her arms, and just stared at me. She seemed angry, so I said, "Tell me what your impression of this project is." She glared at me: "I have no idea why we are doing this. I have been here seventeen years and I do not need any training. I do not like it and I am not sure I even like you."

I had a choice to get defensive or find a way to break the ice—I chose the latter. I said, "Janet, I feel like we are going to become best friends just based on this short interaction—maybe we could socialize sometime soon." She thought I was nuts as she fought back her laughter. I then used that to my advantage. I said, "See, they were wrong—you do have a sense of humor." She lost it…uncontrollably breaking out in laughter.

I had her where I wanted her—the defenses were down and I knew it was not personal. She was scared and justifiably so. Nobody had ever coached her and this program represented changes that people often want to avoid. I said, "Janet, I really appreciate how you feel but I promise you, coaching is not painful. If anything, it's more like what we just experienced (sharing a good laugh)." She said, "Tim, we are all scared if we do not perform, we will lose our jobs." I said, "Janet, if they wanted to fire you, they would. They do not need to spend money on coaching to do that, so if anything, firing people defies logic." She agreed.

As the months progressed, I knew I had to do one major thing when coaching Janet: I had to acknowledge her strengths, which only further opened her mind to those areas where she needed to improve. The critical thing early on was the language I used—I NEVER said, "Here is an area, Janet, where you really stink." Rather, I would say, "One area I would share with you…" or "One observation I would like you to consider…"

As time progressed, Janet actually asked for the feedback, versus having me offer the feedback. Here was a woman in her fifties who took on training as a byproduct of her regular job. She was doing product training in front of one hundred people at a time. This was the same woman who had a fear of change; within fifteen months, she was doing stand-up training, which she had never done before. She had NEVER done stand-up speaking or training in her life.

Result:
Fifteen months after starting the coaching program, Janet was promoted and nearly doubled her salary at a time when most people simply received cost-of-living raises. The moral

is: if you find ways as a coach to gain common ground but challenge people as well as reward them, you will create results.

5. Down Economy Client

One manufacturing client sold to dealers and was in the midst of an industry downturn. The industry was down about 12 percent, but we knew we needed to coach the staff to overcome this. The team was nervous, as rumors ran rampant within the company about possible layoffs. We took an innovative approach to challenging employees to overcome their fears to hit the team's sales goal.

The approach we took used all of the coaching methods. First, each employee had to start each day reading some form of motivation or inspiration. Then all employees would get together for fifteen minutes every morning and afternoon. The objective was to have each group discuss what objections they were experiencing and what response they were using successfully. Finally, the team got together twice a week to discuss how it created success and what challenges they were still experiencing.

In summary, we framed the techniques and activities so the employees had to think positively to complete the activities. We structured coaching assignments for them to first report how they were creating success—the only way to complete the assignments was to be successful. The team worked together for four straight months—with little or no management involvement—to pursue successes and overcome challenges. The moral of this story is: structure activities that focus on creating success during difficult times.

Result:

For the last three programs, sales increased 22 percent, 31 percent, and 74 percent, respectively, when few people thought we would ever hit the base goals. We never held a workshop or any other type of traditional training. Instead, we used peer-to-peer coaching to accelerate practice sessions among the staff. The efforts built confidence and dialogue to solve selling challenges on a daily basis—staff had little or no management input during the sessions.

6. The Rough and Tough Crowd

One major manufacturing client had a team of people who provided technical support to customers. The support centered on building custom parts for equipment. The introverted staff wanted only to e-mail customers, versus interaction with customers on the phone. The customers were angry about this limited customer service interaction.

The approach was threefold. First, we extensively coached both department managers on this team about the methods and techniques. Then each employee completed a self-directed learning matrix, which was filled with activities such as reading articles, calling customers, etc. The biggest task in the matrix was to read a book about change and describe what the employees felt they learned about themselves, and what they needed to change. This created a breakthrough for many employees who said things like "We know we need to change." We extensively praised their honesty, thus encouraging their open-minded behavior.

Finally, we conducted weekly group coaching sessions. Each session required employees to come up with one success they had created during a customer interaction. The last thing an employee wants to do is to come to a meeting without anything to offer, but if everyone has the same task, no one could complain. Initially, when people presented their successes we focused on rewarding their efforts. The fact is desired results will not occur until effort becomes a constant activity.

Results:

Customers engaged with the company to the point that within fifteen months of the program's start, they were requesting staff to attend their annual service meeting. This request was in direct contrast to their history.

Summary

The goal of our case studies is not to impress you, but to show that coaching can be a specific methodology to drive performance and address real-world challenges. We hope our case studies will help people realize if they have a plan to coach and stick to that plan, results will come. The main objective of coaching is to coach for progress, because results rarely come in short time frames.

How to Start a Coaching Program

Starting a coaching process comes down to each manager making the commitment to enable his or her employees to progress. The process is straightforward:

I. Assessment
    a. The assessment can take two forms:
        i. Observation – managers will know the core areas each employee needs to develop.
        ii. Gap Analysis – the Progress Coaching System uses a rating system to define the level of performance against the defined functional requirements.

II. Design
    a. The Progress Coaching System provides choices. The design process can leverage the gap analysis as well as the observational perspective. The design process allows for managers to pick various coaching approaches keeping their time in perspective. The system allows for coaching to be delivered even if management is not physically present.

III. Coaching Approaches / Types
    a. Among five types of coaching that you can deliver, three do not require management's presence. This enables accelerated performance because it does not

depend solely upon management conducting one-on-one sessions.

IV. Coaching Techniques

a. During any coaching session, it's vital that managers are equipped to deal with reactions and challenges from employees as coaching commences.

V. Validation and Re-evaluation

a. Multiple factors measure the evaluation process—the key is to recognize progress and areas where progress is not being experienced. Here are high-level descriptions that will define opportunities for validating and evaluating a coaching program:

  i. Simple observation

  ii. Score sheets (skill and behavior)

  iii. Tests (knowledge)

  iv. Tracking of learning projects' completion (behavior)

Assessment

The assessment process is critical for one main reason. It gets employees involved early by gaining their input. Also, it defines levels of assessment from the employees' perspectives, the manager's view of the employees, and the gap between the two. These results are then correlated with the value of the specific area being assessed.

There are basic steps to follow when developing an assessment process:

1. List all the aspects of performance you desire (functional requirements)
2. Then categorize them into the Four Tiers of Learning:

Skills

Knowledge

Behavior

Creativity

> Note: Here are some key questions to ask for each tier of learning:
>   - "What knowledge does an employee need to do this job effectively?"
>   - "What skills does an employee need to do this job effectively"?
>   - "What behaviors does an employee need to exhibit to do this job effectively"?

The following functional rating scale helps both the employee and manager evaluate where they see performance levels relating to the employee. The rating scale is useful because it's specific to a level of performance, versus an interpretative scale such as "excellent, very good, good…"

0 - No concept or ability.

1 - Recognizes the concept, but cannot demonstrate any real ability or understanding.

2 - Knows the concept and can demonstrate ability/ understanding at a basic level.

3 - Demonstrates level of expertise—answers most questions or provides demonstration of ability.

4 - Can teach/demonstrate without flaw or hesitation to answer questions—absolute expert.

In addition to the functional ratings, it's critical to define the value drivers per functional requirement. This allows for coaching to be done only in areas of highest importance. For example, cold calling would have a higher value driver than the value for a customer service rep. Essentially, what is the value of the functional requirement as it relates to the job?

3 - Vital

2 - Needed, but not vital

1 - It would be nice, but not needed

NA - Not applicable

Sample Assessment Grid (Go to www.salesprogress.com/ coachingtools to download an assessment sheet you can use)

This table shows how an assessment looks when completed:

Functional Requirement	Employee Rating	Manager Rating	Gap	Value Driver
Cold Calling	3	1	-2	3
Handling Price Objections	2	1	-1	3
Product XYZ Demonstration	3	2	-1	3
Product ABC Demonstration	2	2	0	3

- Essentially, the gaps are created by subtracting the manager ratings from the employee ratings. It's important to note the manager and employee will not agree, but that's not the objective. The objective is to identify areas where there is a gap, which serves as the basis to close the gap together. This breeds a cooperative effort between manager and employee.

- Initially, look for gaps with highest value drivers and ascertain the high level areas of needs.

- The results will produce a model to help implement your coaching program.

- There aren't always gaps...sometimes the manager and employee will be in agreement about a developmental need, but the level of performance is not a 3 or 4, where both desire the level to be. Even in agreement, there is opportunity to coach.

Design Sample

Functional Requirement	Employee Rating	Manager Rating	Gap	Value Driver
Cold Calling	3	1	-2	3
Handling Price Objections	2	1	-1	3
Product XYZ Demonstration	3	2	-1	3
Product ABC Demonstration	2	2	0	3

Suggested Design Imperatives

1. Top two gaps – *One-on-One*

2. Next two gaps – *Peer to Peer*

3. Next two gaps – *Group*

4. Rest of the gaps – *Self-Directed Learning*

General Coaching Type Introductions:

Thirty-Second Coaching

- The thirty-second coaching technique is a short, direct, high-energy approach to building and sustaining change with repeatable, short bursts. Keys to success:

1. Be specific to the issue that prompted the coaching feedback.

2. Do NOT mix messages; deliver only that message.

3. If appropriate, gesture with a hand on the shoulder, because it shows an employee you truly care.

4. Use a positive adjective like "fantastic" or "great."

One-on-One

- This is a bi-daily, bi-weekly, and/or weekly scheduled session.

- Each session starts with the previous week's assigned learning project (this is critical to the momentum of the coaching; it challenges the mind of the employee to ascertain if he or she committed).

Group

- Group coaching is usually done weekly.

- This relies on a one-theme concept.

- It requires the group to produce some form of activity (simulation, role-play, group discussion).

Peer to Peer

- Employees coaching one another can open the lines of communication and target areas of development. It also fosters team development while building performance levels.

- The activities for peer-to-peer coaching must be specific and well defined, because employees will often interpret what they want to do.

SDL

- This activity is a "prescribed" activity where the employee conducts an activity and reports back to his or her manager.
- This is often used when a manager is too busy and/or has too many employees.

Once the assessment is completed, it's vital to create a coaching plan. The plan can use one or all of the coaching types (the types will be discussed in greater detail later). The following is a sample coaching plan for an employee who needs to increase his or her cold call performance:

Sample Coaching Plan

Specific Area of Development	Cold Calling & Creating Unique "Openers"		
Frequency	*Coaching Session*	*Suggested Activity*	*Learning Project*
Week One	1) Review expectations of the targeted performance area. 2) Challenge employee to come up with two creative business openers to be used in the real world.	Have the employee write down the names of companies where he or she felt successful and why - a journal of sorts. Repeat for 4 to 6 weeks.	Bring in two examples by client name where you used a successful cold call opener.

Week Two	Review learning project and role-play out loud or discuss what would be done differently.	Have the employee write down the names of companies where he or she felt successful and why - a journal of sorts. Repeat for 4 to 6 weeks.	Bring in two examples by client name where you used a successful cold call opener.
Week Three	Review learning project and role-play out loud or discuss what would be done differently.	Have the employee write down the name of companies where he or she felt successful and why - a journal of sorts. Repeat for 4 to 6 weeks.	Bring in two examples by client name where you used a successful cold call opener.

Types of Coaching

I bet you thought all coaching was one-on-one with an employee—this is where our methodology is different from others.

Five Types of Coaching

  1. – Thirty-Second

  2. – One-on-One

  3. – Peer to Peer

  4. – Group

  5. – SDL

One-on-One Coaching

This should be no more than forty-five–sixty minutes weekly, usually with one to two actual sessions. Each session should be filled with activities that the employees perform (role-play, discussion, teach back, demonstrate, etc.). There should be no more than one or two areas covered, and these issues should be major and targeted for three to six months—this ensures change has not only started, but has cemented itself.

Peer to Peer

Always have an assignment due at the end of a peer-to-peer session, such as staff e-mailing what happened during the session, or filling out scoring sheets on how they saw their partner do in a role-play or assignment. This ensures the activity was done and there are some metrics. Peer-to-peer coaching helps facilitate good teamwork among employees, and it ensures that performance is being improved—even without management attendance.

Group

Group coaching is NOT a time for lecture but a time for employees to perform some action. Activities include discussion, role-plays, etc.—scoring sheets can be used. Group coaching is designed to help improve a performance area the entire staff needs to address.

SDL

The tasks within SDL should be fifteen minutes or less. The design of SDL is to have staff complete short activities within a defined area to help reinforce the learning in small segments. For example, "Build two creative openers for your cold calls and e-mail them to your manager."

Customer Service Rep SDL Sample

Learning Tasks	Task/ Activity Time	Coach Sign Off or Staff Person Check Off	Point Value	Staff Person as Contact Person
Basics				
Take "Handling Objections" course from Sales Progress and e-mail your manager two things you learned about yourself of where you feel you could get better	15 minutes		2	Any employee
Find two articles on Google on "How to Handle Price Objections" and e-mail your manager two things you learned and what you will apply	15 minutes		2	Self
Name a client you experienced an objection with and describe how you handled it	15 minutes		3	Self

Summary

No matter the coaching type, the employee should be taking some action...As managers, we need to be creative when designing a coaching program.

"Four Tiers of Learning" Coaching Methods

A. Knowledge

- Evaluation Methods – demonstration, tests.
- Coaching or Self-Directed Methods:
  1. **_Show Me_** – this method has the student showing how to do something that would require knowledge, such as product knowledge.
  2. **_Demo and Receive Feedback_** – this method has the student actually doing a demo where knowledge is required.
  3. **_Teach the Teacher_** – a great method is having the student experience role reversal, where he or she has to teach a topic or knowledge set—"to know something is to have the ability to teach it."

B. Skills

- Evaluation Methods – role-playing, tests, observation.
- Coaching or Self-Directed Methods:
  1. **_Show Me_** – this method has the student showing how to do something that would require skills such as closing, presentation, etc.
  2. **_Demonstrate and Q and A_** – this is similar to Show Me, but also incorporates Q and A to quantify knowledge required to do the skill.
  3. **_Role-Play_** – critical to the development of any skill. A person must practice skills like asking open-ended questions, listening, etc.

4. <u>*Act As If...*</u> – this is a form of modeling. It helps employees by having them mimic or act out the skill as if they had been doing it for years. For example, a student who is scared of making cold calls may act as if he or she is a million-dollar-per-year salesperson on the phone to facilitate the feeling of what it's like to actually do the cold calls.

C. Behavior

- Evaluation Methods – role-playing, tests.
- Coaching or Self-Directed Methods:
    1. <u>*Absurd Exaggeration*</u> – this has the students act well beyond the required behavior to help them realize the required behavioral change is not as difficult as they thought.
    2. <u>*Self-Analysis*</u> – this is an abridged version of 360-degree feedback. Have three fellow employees write down what they see in a person's behavior and have the employee analyze what is valid and not so valid. This is used as a starting point.
    3. <u>*Watch and Reflect*</u> – this is simple observation with additional work, such as documenting another person's positive behavioral attributes (walking with energy, body language, etc.).
    4. <u>*Question Back*</u> – this helps employees truly own an issue by not giving them the answer they seek. For example, if they ask how to do something, a "question back" response would be "What do you think should be done?"

D. Creativity

- Evaluation Methods – role-playing, tests.
- Coaching or Self-Directed Methods:

    1. ___Non-Industry Explanation___—to generate some creative energy, have an employee come up with solutions to a problem by using adjectives from a non-similar industry. For example, if an employee is confused about a client's needs, you can ask him or her to play the role of football coach and use some football analogies to solve the problem.

    2. ___Brainstorm___ – this is the most common technique. Ask an employee to lead or present a whiteboard presentation.

    3. ___"What Would You Do?"___ – prompt the employee with constant versions of the question "What would you do?" In addition, this technique can be done at varying degrees, by adding questions like, "If you were the client, what would you want the salesperson to do?" The goal is to get the employee to see the issue from different perspectives.

Coaching Techniques

Coaching techniques are those techniques to be used within the coaching process and type of coaching. For example, whether you are conducting a private one-on-one or group coaching session, managers will need techniques to drive performance.

1. **Question Back**

   Often, employees will ask a manager how to do something while that manager is on the way to a meeting. The manager will simply give the answer, so he or she can move on to the meeting. In essence, this interaction develops a dependency on behalf of the employee.

   Question Back prompts the employee to own the situation. This technique has the leader asking the employee "What do you think you should do?" or "If I were not here right now, what would you do?"

2. **Third-Party Observation**

   This technique helps people realize their fear or apprehension with completing a task by admitting their fears. The technique lowers their defenses by using a third-party observation. For example, if an employee is hesitating to complete something or admit the challenge, a manager might ask, "If the president were here right now, what would his or her impression of you be?" The employee immediately thinks about that third party versus ways to get out of answering the question.

3. Hypothetical

This technique is similar to third-party observations, but we replace the third-party element with the word "hypothetically." For example, if an employee were demonstrating a lack of skills in an area, the manager could state, "Hypothetically, if I were I to tell you needed to improve your skills, how would you react?" The trick is to use the word that gives a false sense of security—the employee feels the manager is not really asking the question. Why? Because he or she used the word "hypothetically."

4. Silence is Your Friend

When coaching employees, it can be uncomfortable for managers as much as employees. When a tough issue is being discussed, it's imperative—when asking an employee a question—that he or she answers. Sometimes we get uncomfortable and make it easy for employees. Silence is one of the most powerful techniques if used properly. When asking employees questions that are tough or to the point, let silence be your friend—it's more uncomfortable for them than you.

5. Absurd Exaggeration

This technique is exactly what it sounds like. You exaggerate the point to an absurd level to ensure your point is made. For example, if an employee is being negative and your efforts have been exhausted, this technique can really be productive. An example might be, "Tim, you are so inspiring...have you thought about writing a motivational book? People must be proud to be around you." Now, this is aggressive, but at times employees need to see who they are or how they are perceived.

6. Rating Questions

This is a great technique for knowledge, skill, and behavior-based coaching challenges. The Rating Question technique really gets the employee to get in touch with what he or she needs to do.

Skill-Based Example: "On a scale of 1 to 10, with 10 being outstanding and 1 being terrible, how would you rate your ability to close customers from a skill perspective?"

If they answer below 5, simply ask, "Why?"

If they answer above 5, ask, "What do you feel you need to work on to move toward a 9 or 10?"

Knowledge-Based Example: "On a scale of 1 to 10, with 10 being outstanding and 1 being terrible, how would you rate your ability to teach customers our new product?"

If they answer above 5, ask, "What do you feel you need to work on to move toward a 9 or 10?"

Behavior-Based Example: "On a scale of 1 to 10, with 10 being 'no fear' and 1 being 'fearful,' how you would rate your fear to close customers from a skill perspective?"

If they answer above 5, ask "What do you feel you need to work on to move toward a 9 or 10?"

Note: If employees really think they are at a level of 9 or 10 and you know they are not, here are some questions to further attempt to have them see reality:

- "What do you base that on?"

- "Based on your response, would it be safe to assume you will achieve 100 percent success (this really pins them down on validating their responses)?"

7. **Demo Me**
   A great technique to develop a type of skill is to have the employee demonstrate it. All too often, we get our employees in a room for a meeting and tell or show what they need to do in regard to a skill—the problem is we do not validate that they have the skill. The ability to demonstrate this helps accelerate skill development.

8. **Teach the Teacher**
   Similar to Demo Me is Teach the Teacher, but this technique is geared more for knowledge. Many organizations conduct product training in workshop settings teaching the features and benefits, all the while assuming employees have a firm grasp on the knowledge. The only way to gauge knowledge level is to either test for it, or have the ability to teach it back.

Note: the techniques can be used within a coaching session or as a learning project between coaching sessions. Here are two examples of using the techniques within and outside of a coaching session:

1. During a coaching session, a manager may ask the employee to teach the product features, pretending he or she is a new employee.

2. After a coaching session, a manager may ask an employee to come back next week prepared to demonstrate the top ten features of a software package as if the manager were a novice user.

These examples are simple but they put the onus on the employee's shoulders.

Coaching Language

When coaching people, it is vital you use language that is conducive to learning. Most managers' language immediately puts up barriers to the learning process, without the managers even knowing it. Asking questions is critical to the process:

Behavioral Based Questions	How do you feel when you are doing that or experiencing it? On a scale of 1 to 10 with 10 being very nervous, how would rate your anxiety? (A great question to ask afterward would be "What could I do to help you become more comfortable?")
Skill Based Questions	How would you rate your level of proficiency? (give rating scale)
Knowledge Based Questions	If I were to ask you to teach me, how accurate do you feel your teaching would be and why?
Creative Based Questions	• Help me understand... • What do you think would help you get more ... (name the skill, knowledge or behavioral issue — fear, anxiety, nervousness) • What help do you need and what role would you like me to play? (You are asking for them to ask for coaching help - this opens the mind and makes the coaching less intrusive.)

- Do NOT use words like "wrong," "right," or "bad" (you are coaching to develop progress, not results initially).

- When getting employees to look at their performance, offer phrases like "one observation I had was…" or "I would encourage you to look at it from this perspective…" The phrases are designed to keep employees' minds open to learning versus feeling defensive. All too often, people lead with "What you did wrong was…" Who in his or her right mind feels positive and consistently open to learning when hearing this?

Measuring Coaching Success: Validate and Re-evaluate

Use score sheets, scorecards, and dedicated observation to ascertain a specific understanding of performance strengths and areas for improvement.

Area	_1_	_2_	_3_	_4_	_5_
# of closed questions					
# of open questions					
# of benefits delivered					
# of positive adjectives					
# of interruptions					

Area	_Poor_	_Fair_	_Good_	_Very Good_	_Outstanding_
Energy					
Active listening					
Understood customer's needs					
Maintained energy from start to finish					
Stayed focused on customer's issues					

Sample Factual Score Sheet

Factual Score Sheet

Name of Employee _____
Date   _____

Performance Area	*1*	*2*	*3*	*4*	*5*
Open-ended questions					
Positive adjective used					
Benefits delivered direct to customer needs					
Number of cross-sell attempts					
Number of up-sell attempts					
Number of closing attempts					

Notes:

Sample Presentation Score Sheet

Presentation Score Sheet

Performance Area	*Could teach or demo flawlessly*	*Needs some work, but it's not a major area of concern*	*Average, if practiced or worked on, could make significant impact to their bottom line*	*Absolutely sub-par, if practiced or worked on, could make major impact to their bottom line*
Presenter was prepared				
Captured attention in first 60 seconds				
Got audience engaged within first three minutes				
Presentation was persuasive, not a boring talk				
Presenter delivered case studies & evidence to support business offerings				
Maintained eye contact				
Maintained positive body language				
Demonstrated great energy & enthusiasm				
Set stage for next meeting with confidence & next dates				

Also download forms in Word format at www.salesprogress.com/coachingtools

Building Your Coaching Ability

Coaching—like anything else—takes practice. Yes, it's a change for most managers, because of the simple fact that it's easier to tell staff what to do and not engage—there's no risk in telling staff what do to. Nor is there exposure on behalf of the manager.

Also, make sure to use the charts, exercises and other resources available through this book and on our Web site.

Practice activities—how to start:

1. First, adopt one simple principle that most managers will struggle with while trying to become coaches: If you are telling them, you are dictating. If you are asking them, they are part of the process.

2. Start with one person. Define his or her greatest area of need and what tier of learning the challenge resides within: knowledge, skills, behavior, or creativity.

3. Pick "low-hanging" fruit. Select topics that will allow the person to have immediate success. This will prompt him or her to have a positive association with coaching.

Sustaining a Coaching Culture

Building an organization structure that sustains the coaching movement can impact the organization's bottom line. There is a process to enabling an organization to support the Progress Coaching movement:

1. Conduct a best practices session—learn and share great coaching tips and procedures.

2. Have managers attend a coaching workshop—hone the skills needed to become a top-notch coach.

3. Conduct regularly scheduled practice sessions—use role-plays and case studies to boost coaching skills.

4. Develop Management Coaching Commitment Plans (get document at www.salesprogress.com/coachingtools)—paint a detailed picture of your future coaching strategies.

5. Obtain executive-level support—every leader needs to show that the organization is unified in support of the coaching movement.

Resources

Sales Progress LLC has created a site where you can gain free access to our coaching forms.

Master Coaching Cheat Sheet (also download at www.salesprogress.com/coachingtools)

Tier of Learning	Assessment Methods	Evaluation Methods	Coaching Method
1. Skill	❖ Role-playing & scoring ❖ Act it out ❖ Observe & score ❖ Simple observation	❖ Role-playing & scoring ❖ Observation	❖ Show me ❖ Demonstrate & receive feedback ❖ Teach the teacher ❖ Role-play & receive feedback
2. Knowledge	❖ Test ❖ Teach the teacher	❖ Test ❖ Demonstration	❖ E-mail & explain what you have learned ❖ Teach the teacher ❖ Read & write what you learned ❖ Present case study & ask "What would you do?"
3. Behavioral	❖ Role-playing ❖ Skit ❖ Structured experiences	❖ Surveys ❖ Subjective rating	❖ Absurd exaggeration ❖ Self-analysis ❖ Watch and reflect ❖ Question back
4. Creative	❖ Brainstorming	❖ Self-analysis ❖ Group	❖ Non-industry explanation

Summary

Sales Progress LLC works with a variety of organizations in developing coaching managers and cultures. We provide our instruction in a variety of innovative ways. The key is to realize you have choices:

- First, there are five coaching types.

- There are four types of learning.

- There are eight basic techniques to use within the coaching sessions.

If you lack time, use self-directed or peer-to-peer coaching. If your team shares a common performance need, use group coaching. If one employee really has a major performance need, one-on-one may be the best route. Again, the point of this book is to let you know you have choices. If you combine some of the methods and use the right techniques, you can really accelerate the development of employees.

Finally, be patient—coaching will take time for you and the employees. Change is not something that happens overnight. It will take you time, but once understood and mastered, performance development will never be an issue with your staff.

In addition, create a plan to start a coaching plan within your department or organization. It's simple to create the plan, and sticking to it will accelerate your coaching success.

Biography

Tim Hagen founded Sales Progress, a SaleBuilder Marketing company, in 1997. His entrepreneurial career began in college leading to positions in sales, sales management, and sales training for small and large corporations, and eventually ownership of several training companies. He possesses a unique combination of hands-on experience, academics, and innovative insight to solve the industry's most common challenges. Tim holds a bachelor's degree in Adult Education and Training from the University of Wisconsin, Milwaukee.

Made in the USA
Charleston, SC
07 May 2011